# MOMMY'S TIME-OUT

## Adult Coloring Book

# SWEAR WORDS

# EDITION

Jamesa Lynn Leyhe

This book contains an array of inappropriate, Sassy, and yet delightfully beautiful swear words. Yet they are designed to be classy!

Dedicated to all the mommy's out there that are overworked, unpaid and just STRESSED THE FUCK OUT.
We have to stick together!!
Much love to my besties Whit, Sam and Kita for all their encouragment.

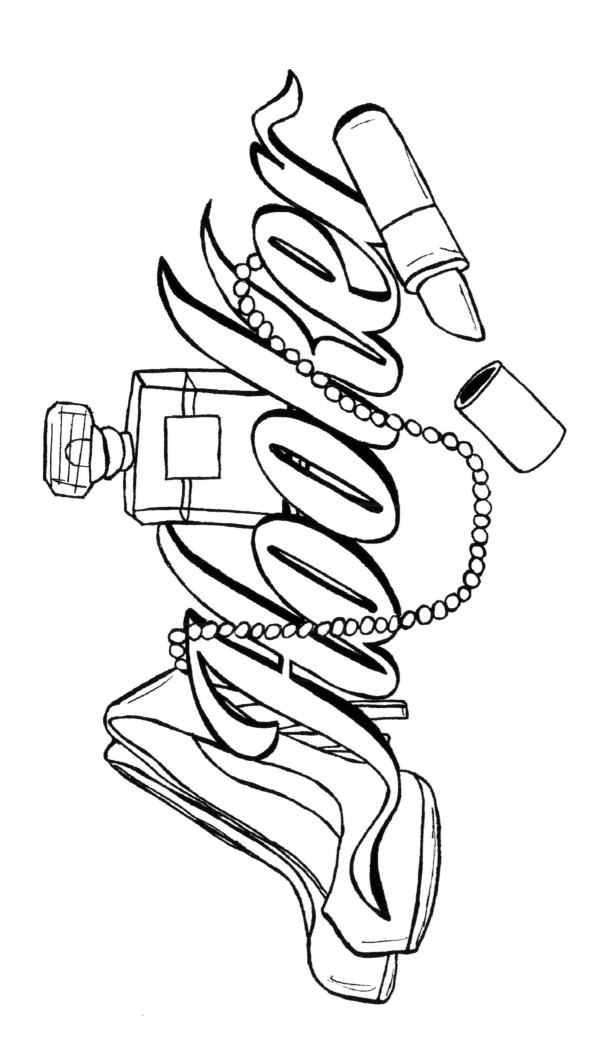

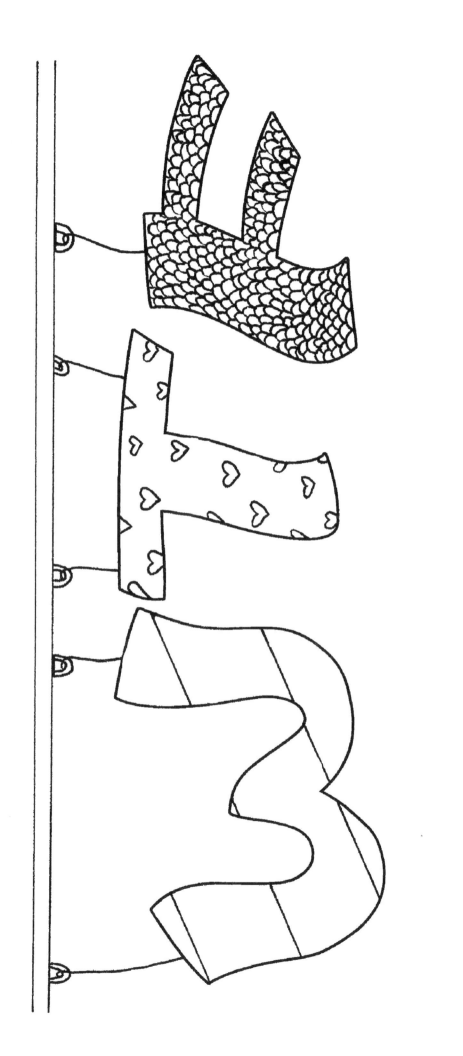

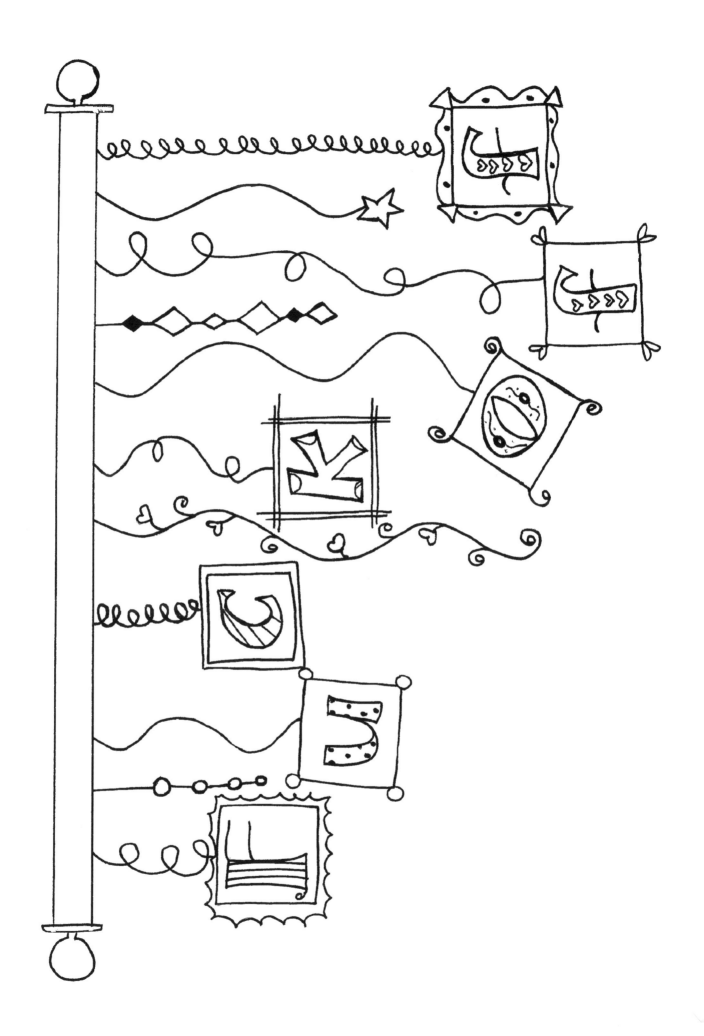

# Color Check Page

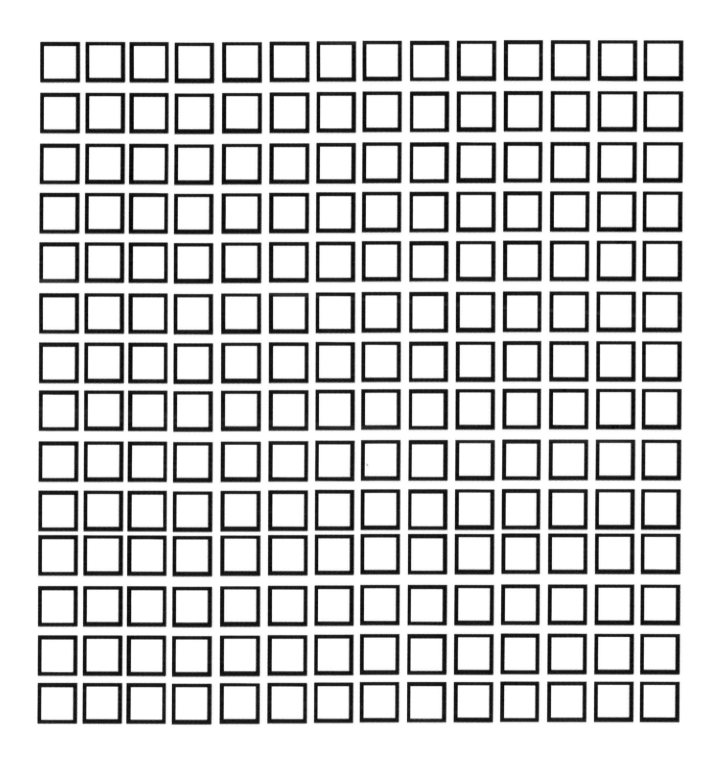

# Blotter Page

Tear this page out and use it between
your coloring sheets to avoid bleeding

# Join me at

www.facebook.com/groups/TimeOut.Coloring.Books

Share your work and Join for
upcoming details and free giveaways
of future books.

Coming Soon

SAMPLE

from

Mommy's Time-Out

Fuck my day

Coloring Book

Made in the USA
San Bernardino, CA
25 April 2016